Ghost of the Eye

poems by

Roselyn Elliott

Finishing Line Press
Georgetown, Kentucky

Ghost of the Eye

ACKNOWLEDGMENTS

I would like to thank the following journals for publication of individual poems:

The Cumberland River Review, " Night Rain"
BLUELINE, A literary magazine dedicated to the spirit of the Adirondacks,
        "Crows Along the River Trail"
diode poetry journal, "At my Mother's House, October of Her 88th Year," "Ghost
        of the Eye," "Blue Moon," "Notes Holding Us Tight to the World"
Streetlight Magazine, "Letter to the Body"
The Comstock Review, "While We Sleep" under the title "New Year"

Publisher: Leah Maines

Editor: Christen Kincaid

Cover Art: https://pixabay.com; CCO Public Domain images

Author Photo: Lester Bares

Cover Design: Elizabeth Maines

Printed in the USA on acid-free paper.
Order online: www.finishinglinepress.com
        also available on amazon.com

Author inquiries and mail orders:
Finishing Line Press
P. O. Box 1626
Georgetown, Kentucky 40324
U. S. A.

Table of Contents

For my siblings: Gloria, Eleanor, Janet, Alfred Jr.,
Frances, Helen, Steven, and Barbara

Fog and Fighter Jets

Fighter jets whine, slice sky
over this beach city. Fog presses wet, gray
against hotel walls and windows.
Surf never-ending is out there somewhere.
Peace is a long sweater unraveling
above the sea, its thread a contrail
between clouds. And through the soup,
pilots train their silver toys straight up,
then arc, transecting the gulls' paths.
That buzz-saw wail of descent
assaults us, but this is fake war, without
the thud, the boom, without craters of regret.
We came to play, but the racket traps us,
in a world longing for light. Here, we wait
inside our room, burning for a view,
a wind blowing inland or out to sea,
lifting the shroud off ships, wait, to hear
nothing but breakers lapping the strand.

Night Rain

Gray pearls roll down the heights
stinging the world, soaking feathers
of gray birds, clusters of milkweed,
pulling wiry fronds to earth.
The smallest of pendants
in a necklace of clear droplets
cling to the lip of a clay pot.
Detritus of leaves and insect wings
wash into old sand.

Now a measured drumming
on the skylight. What can we do
but rise to meet it? Leave in the bed
the weight of long days, rise
through spaces between cells
of skin, between fibers of muscle,
rise and enter each drop's
unrelenting dispersal of time.

Until the sky takes hold of everything,
soaks the tapestry whose threads we are,
whose intervals between threads we are,
fibers woven across each other:
green beside black, over washed red.
Filaments of tight harmonious
motifs grip us without reprieve.
Barely able to breathe, we escape
into dreams, pretend to be deer,
step out of the pattern, bound away.

Crows along the River Trail

We walk on sand left by the flood,
step over rivulets from the weeping cliff.

Deep in the woods five caws begin.
On the opposite bank, three caws reply.

White blackberry blossoms arc beside us.
We trample leaves of lily rinsed with mud.

Four caws respond from the woods.
We don't know the code, but we know

the flood rose at night, quickly,
a breathless runner pounding from behind,

cracking branches, pulling a full-grown
hickory into its churn. Black water

swept wrens in their nests downstream,
rapids stood on their haunches and roared.

The crows were silent until morning.

Ghost of the Eye

Tonight, flying home at dusk, among
a bevy of souls in this long bullet
bucking the jet stream, we pass through soft
pink-lavender sunset. I turn my head quickly
to the right, and catch for a second
the long remaining tail of yellow light
left over from the flare inside my eye last year.

Oh, life, carry us through our flashes
        of astonishment without harm—

Hurtling across firmament, faith stretched
across fabric of space, we enter a gray mist
so like a thin specter, a certain coolness
comes to the skin, to the mood, but then,
I see that old companion: brown shadow
in the left periphery, sometimes a small brown dog
lifting onto its hind feet, pawing the air,
now, a long, languid cloud promising rain.

Summer Lights,
A Meditation

Fireflies seed the backyard
your first evening away for work.
The trees and underbrush are alive
with this party. Choreographed to attract
a mate, or prey, each one emits its green flare
the second another switches off. And this sultry
June evening, the private universe of my right eye
showers my vision with commas,
half-moons, parallel gnats dancing
to retinal lightning. At the window
I turn my head quickly, catch
the next shape, the next. Eye flashing
with each small shift, floaters collide
with fireflies, and I remember you'll be gone
a week, reading papers, your eyes straining
with students' cursive. I picture you
bent over the table of notebooks,
think of your patience in all things
all these years, even when I don't see
what you mean, or when I don't look
at you long enough. Fireflies
between trees, pierce the humid dusk
with yellow beads, green stars
lingering into the night.

Cycle of Hope

We are paper leaves borne on thin breath.
Throats thicken, voices rasp, eye lashes

scratch. Memories of afternoon's slow,
soft precipitation, cloying humidity

shrink as cambium recedes, trees waste,
their low branches filled with squirrels,

flaccid from months of heat. Confused
young jays plunge wildly on their way

to desiccation. Pain: bone-scraping-bone,
joint pain, tooth pain, mourning doves

fluttering upward-to-salvation pain.
Skin and lungs slough cell by cell

into static air. There is nothing left to say.
No will to reach past suffering.

Our diminutive future flickers, its song lost
on the dry tongue of a morning thrush.

Yet, near the sea, a woman sitting in front
of her house, shelling green peas, imagines

palm trees in holy flexion before a laden cloud.
A boy walking a village street sees a slight gust

invert the underside of leaves, an anger
collecting itself, pulling renegade waves

into charged air. The tempest swells
across a mackerel sky. The eye, at nightfall,

envelopes a stratus cloud, Whirling its brawn,
the cyclone howls its power home.

The Effect of Light on the Brain of a Blue-Winged Warbler

Joyous at the edge of the forest, she's snatching
infant crickets, mealy bugs, crunching katydids
to her *tsi tsi tsi* song. Just returned from the Argentine,

she's all hungry for caterpillars and sex, her eye
trained for her male, presently hanging upside down
on the branch above her. They've returned today

because their supra-chias-matic nucleus, nestled
tightly above the juncture where visions shoot
along their optic nerves, stirred their appetites

for fat and travel, creating a restlessness
that shudders down each feather, until they
fly and fly and fly. Before sunrise a week ago,

this pair rose through the light of May and joined
a wave of their kind, northbound. Each year
they reappear at the edge of your backyard, because

their eyes hold twice the rods and cones we use,
each with its own droplet of oil, though we
can only imagine the colors they see.

As they followed Earth's magnetic lines,
you listened for her call, just as now your vision
strives to spy her flashes of blue between leaves,

before twilight absorbs the world.

Letter to the Body

If only you were the pure self,
we would not have to bargain or pray,
offer up good deeds for relief of pain, or
apologies for spasms and expectorations.
The cells could absorb and discharge at leisure.
Whatever waste washes ashore in the brain
or in the heart, would, without shame,
increase the one being. No struggle to justify,
no explaining we're really much better
than our hunched back, our protuberances,
just the material presence, occupying space,
insular and detaching, floating away
for a day on the sea's silver face, returning
to endless pleasures of the anatomy.

In the Labyrinth of Passion

In my lower spine, that cold throb is rage
uncoiling, forgotten affronts amassed
in sacral joints, waiting to disappear me
in the furious smoke of celestial ire.

My new reluctance to reach for the brass ring
is the shortening band in my left shoulder
holding sorrow in check as I watch my mother
labor through her deep senescence.

The soft light of my cat, Alexander, who
stretched every night on the bed beside me,
whose spirit my arms absorbed as I held him
in death, mitigates arthritic stabs.

Deep in my belly, in a labyrinth of passion,
surrounded by pulsating great vessels,
deep among ancient questions and scars,
desire hunts for a door to the world.

The body knows who lies awake
through years of sleepless nights, knows
whose diligent pulse sounds the way.

In the Cool Swirl

Who might she have been, gray shadow
blowing across my sister's living room?
Living dust, visible energy, a fleeting
twilight, seen by some of us, but
not others, easily mistaken
for holiness, but not quite holy.
She lingers, brushes our bodies, watches
us fold towels, rushes away. My sister
says, at night, a fist knocks the wall
behind her bed and she knocks back.

Who did I see, too soon separated
from her blood and thirst, caught here
in the cool swirl of spirit holding on
to time? On each visit I long to see her,
yet hope not to see her, fearful
of soaring past the rock bridge,
returning formless, nameless,
a gusty breeze disturbing window blinds,
a catchy rhythm knocking the sill.

At my Mother's House, October of her 88th Year

Look at the light. Look between the trees
    where branches overlap. Stippled
        green and yellow, foliage gleams

a few seconds silver. Across the road,
    where the first house stood,
        burnished orange has blasted

one side of a conical maple. The beech is flying
    its cadmium flags, that will cling
        all winter. Hemlocks sway.

Staghorn sumac browned by frost,
    holds its furry seeds teetering
        at the edge of over-ripe.

In through this raised bedroom window,
    a breeze wanders away from its mother
        the wind, which belongs nowhere.

Its warm gusts have rushed off the great lake,
    whirling a magnificent cape,
        undulating above lively marshes,

tilted between ocher and bronze,
    sliding down the vertical blue.
        Undeterred, it enters this bedroom,

ruffles blank pages, awakens
    summer's somnolent flies, stirs
        eddies of dust, each mote

a memory untethered, drifting
in a ray of variegated light,
that sweeps over me, half-asleep,

half-covered, nerve endings alive,
restless and unwilling to settle
into the comfortable bed.

Blue Moon

You were the happy one with curls,
an easy giggle the rest of us envied,
pride of our pack of siblings.
Sister, why did you go away?
Before your voice went missing,
your smile drew us into a green park.
Our braided laughter climbed the sycamores,
drifted across lazy afternoons.
Today, inside me, only a white circle
is left from your busy erasing.
Here, at the hot end of summer,
the molting jays and tanagers
crack and nibble hard seeds while we wait
for autumn's cool relief. Tomorrow
is the second full moon this month.
I wonder if the birds will lift toward it,
or will they keep concealed under the hedges,
continue this long diminishment?

Released

for Michelle

Had the fog not risen slowly from the lake
all day, covering the countryside, fur-like,
clinging, had she not

been wrapped in her own fog of happiness
and gratitude with the news her father
would survive—(father with a failing heart,

father forgiven, alive. Such possibilities)—
the story might be different. Had she not
driven through that milky bisque

toward the house where her child waited,
a route engraved behind her eyes,
steering inside the fog down the empty

country road, the day would not have been
remembered long for weather. But the crash,
which to her, probably was silent

took away the car so suddenly
she was outside everything, fluttering
in damp twilight

floating over the lake's white breath
wondering how she would get to the child,
and lost to us all.

Lost

Still-life with plums is not a bad way to start morning.
Memories catch on a leaf and fall forever.

Longing for gestational sleep, you wander among
embryonic thoughts, hungry for language, forgetting

how to converse with the world. Chronology sprung,
yesterday's laughter rings down a desert valley.

A lone watcher on the mountain remembers the touch
of a lover's soft breath, hardened now to cold wisdom.

Between stones a dahlia quickens, twists toward light.
A sparrow hits the window pane. Cars collide,

a mother disappears. Deep in thought, her child waits
behind branches of plum trees latticed in the night-light

of an old motel, leaves veering like shadows
across cracked asphalt of the parking lot.

Lines for My Sister

They open her heart and find four children inside:
one deceased, one insane, a husband who passed
away building a temple for the multitude who
never came. Sharp tacks in another chamber, the kind
that prick when you cry and gravel your voice, and
a tiny sack of violets tucked away in the chamber
where her daughter waits in her never-ending thirty-fourth
year. A mesh of scars resembling red demons
in her son's brain, robbed her muscle's will to pulse.
The stiffened valve resigned from its job. But
today, from a bovine donor, a substitution is stitched
by the surgeon and her corpuscles flow anew, out into
her arid geography, down through the territory of blue legs
made quick again, into green eyes for glimpsing clear faces,
cleaning her brain to remember friends names, childhood
smells of warm toast, hot chocolate. Out of the fog that
enveloped her daughter on the empty country road,
her broken heart refurbished, she enters the world again.

Notes Holding Us Tight to the World

live in the pause between inhale and exhale,
between fronds of an asparagus-fern
with its one red berry.

A single muscle cell of the heart beats alone,
little solitary god in a laboratory dish
waiting for another of its kind

to thump in synchrony until the small rooms
pulsate a flame continuous and steady:
a star in the blue-black sky.

In deep sleep, the heart flips an extra beat
into the cosmos, then another and another,
beginning an endless journey of lives,

chanting overlapped notes, their feet drumming
an old path above the river's low hymn
footprint into footprint, in perfect time.

Losing Her Blues at the Art Institute of Chicago

She told me how she stared for hours
at Chagall's windows, that afternoon.
Gazing into lapis light, she sank
slowly beyond the leaded glass,
beckoned by his yellow ballerina,
streams of violin inside her mind.

Guided by the bright dove of peace,
deep into blue ocean, she swam past
the sorrow of all her lifetimes, and awakened
at his fireside, greeted by a translucent angel
holding a spray of bluebells in her hand.

Her lovers of the future had gathered on the roof,
shy and blushing, in their simple blue suits.

Above them paused a confident blue rooster
suspended in thin air. She climbed up there

laughing and conversing with her beaus,
as long-lived fears, her frozen ire,

the apathy, her pain, released themselves
into the blue forever of his glass.

But her train was waiting at the station.

She swam back, above a field of purple leaves,
barely noticing red horses grazing below.

Excavation in Petra

I walk over you. You, gone a thousand years
in layers beneath my feet, spooned
against your mate, wrapped in time's hush,
deep under sun and rock where water
trickles through stone. We dig and sift
day after day to find your rooms
where passion flared. Up here,

it's dusk now. The wind brings night
quickly, cooling my bones.
Fine dust sifts along the stone path
where you walked to meet her,
pulled by scent of spices from her hair.
When she appeared that first time,
did you know the wind's wisdom?

Centuries drifted down this path,
sand filling spaces between questions.
Your priests, your people, the monastery
are buried and silent. The hollow rooms
inside the mountain belie your city thriving here.
Open windows finally disclose how
the sun's ray entered your mind.

Today, the wavering blue light
of a scanner noticed your skeleton.
Time shuddered. This evening's arid breath
against my arm brings an image of someone
walking toward me, hand extended. Then,
it's gone, and there is only science and the night,
only a few camp fires still burning in the desert.

You Come With Light

There is no poem today
picking its way through my dark dreams
of murder and abandonment, except
you, little junco, standing there on the deck rail,
surveying the morning yard below. Only you,
two-toned and fluffed against the cold, head up,
eyes wide. You are livid with hope, it seems.
Your slate and white feathers perfectly placed,
you glide without thinking down to the millet and
corn, to feed among your kind. I watch,
struggling to shake the thick crimes of night.
But, you come with light, forager,
every day, and you are animate, touchable.
In a simple movement of your head you show me
how to gentle the aftermath of fear.

The Shortest Day

The moon is hanging half-way up the sky.

A great blue heron fixed beside the pond,
knows we have seen it. In this ambiguous

light, brushstrokes of gray and brown, a statue,
five feet tall, the great wings folded

in their racks. With one flap, it rises,
widens the layers of feathers. Flat out,

low over dark water, it glides, long legs dangling,
neck curved into a tight S, the soft sounds

of flight, chords of winter music flowing
through us. Then grandeur slows. It lowers

its feet to grasp the little dock, stands to peer
at us under the reluctant sun, where the trees,

are nearly bare, only beech and white oak
holding their rags. This first day after

the longest night, we had intended, the four
of us, to climb the trail, but instead, turned

toward the pond, and paused, wondering
if the sodden brown grass held too much mud.

Interval

The old cat stirs from sleep,
stands, readjusts her skeleton,
rivets her gaze outside. Suffering
for weeks, she still has hunger,
but wants nothing from us now.
Soon she'll slide past the periphery
and enter my husband's left shoulder,
the one she's kneaded all these years.
He'll carry her warmth, but we won't see her
except for the silent flag of her tail
moving along the bedroom wall.
We'll feel her then, walking between lives,
following us room to room,
underfoot for months.

A Torn Page

Airborne, the cat bites
    a swallowtail's wing, runs,
        spits and spits the bitter
            half-moon stuck on its tongue.

The swallowtail hobbles
    sideways, across the afternoon,
        writing a new alphabet
        across the yard.

Its page torn, unable to rise,
    the butterfly lands on Queen Anne's Lace:
        white flower of refuge,
            stalk of sustenance.

Oh, pain of clipped wing,
    futility, exhaustion.
        Oh, spoiled day, no ladder
            to the sky. Still, it refuses

to sink, or swoon. Half the wing
    is gone, will not grow back,
        but there is time, still
            enough space to write the story.

Ten O'Clock in the Morning

Complex enough to baffle squirrels,
tall enough to tempt the owl,
this altar, two feeders on a high post,
water trough below,
is our unintended offering
to the sharp-shinned hawk
watching from the wooden fence.

This cold autumn day,
she lobs herself between hickories,
unerring for the feeder.
Legs extended, wings thrashing
in reverse thrust, her claws reach
to seize and puncture
one red finch, motionless
on the tube of seeds, but
she misses, thus permitting
the finch to fly
into its next moment, the only one
it cares about, hungry
as it is for the safety
of these woods.

It opens into pure flight,
disappears into a cedar tree,
the hawk already balanced
again on the wooden fence.

Winter Solstice Afternoon

A cocoon flaps in the wind, corner of the house,
dry as its dwellers' dream of wings.

Cherry trees clack in the face of shurring beech.
Pines cross swords, quarrel with the wind.

In false dusk, a pileated pounds decaying oak.
Bluebird flits away. Coreopsis shrivels.

We live in a dark time. Crows in the side yard
march three abreast over corn stubble

into the shadow of a tall hickory,
splayed like three fingers on the yard.

Neighbors' houses blur into fog shrouding
purple mountains. Buzzards drift over the field.

But, inside the house, before a glowing stove,
I coax sleep. A pale corona surrounds my form,

half curled, worm-like, flexed but ready to unfold.

January Bite

Five days to go in this steel-trap.
Even succumbing to sleep changes nothing.
You argue that endless conversation:
"Why? Why didn't you…..?"
Snow solid on the ground, hot soup in the pot.
But when called to dinner no one speaks
around the table. Next day the sun hangs
slack-jawed overhead, and "Don't forget,"
comes out of the snowman's mouth. Five days
you hold on until the moon squanders its haze,
until the check arrives.

While We Sleep

Sheer silence holds night in place.
The oak's stark shadow
refuses to be more than a tall absence
of light between cold rays.
If there are creatures on the floor of the woods,
asleep or scurrying, we don't know,
above them, here in the yellow house,
snuggled into flannel beds—
Whatever stirs under the leaves
scratches its own tunnel, gnaws
to its own pulse and moves on.

Roselyn Elliott was born in Watertown, NY, and grew up in Jefferson County, NY, on a dairy farm with 8 siblings. A graduate of the RN nursing program at the House of the Good Samaritan School of Nursing in Watertown, she worked as a nurse for 27 years in NY State and Virginia. She holds a BA in Cultural History from Mary Baldwin College, and an MFA in Creative Writing, Poetry, from Virginia Commonwealth University. Her poems and essays have appeared in *New Letters, The Cumberland River Review, The Cream City Review, Harpur Palate, The Florida Review, diode poetry journal, ABRAXAS, Blueline, The Comstock Review, Hospital Drive, Streetlight Magazine* and other publications. She is the author of 3 previous poetry chapbooks: *The Separation of Kin* (Blueline—SUNY Potsdam 2006), *At the Center* (Finishing Line Press 2008), and Animals *Usher Us to Grace* (Finishing Line Press 2011).

A Pushcart nominee, she has served as assistant editor for several magazines and has taught at VCU, Piedmont Virginia Community College, The Visual Art Center of Richmond and at WriterHouse in Charlottesville, VA. She resides in Richmond VA with husband, poet Les Bares and 2 cats, Lily and Daisy, a few miles from grandson Arthur W. Elliott and his parents, Mark and Kara.